Great Women in History

# Rosa Parks

by Erin Edison

**Consulting Editor:** Gail Saunders-Smith, PhD

**Consultant:** Georgette M. Norman, Director
Troy University Rosa Parks Museum
Montgomery, Alabama

**CAPSTONE PRESS**
a capstone imprint

Pebble Books are published by Capstone Press,
1710 Roe Crest Drive, North Mankato, Minnesota 56003.
www.capstonepub.com

**Library of Congress Cataloging-in-Publication Data**
Edison, Erin.
  Rosa Parks / by Erin Edison.
      p. cm.—(Pebble books. Great women in history)
  Includes bibliographical references and index.
  ISBN 978-1-62065-071-4 (library binding)
  ISBN 978-1-62065-863-5 (paperback)
  ISBN 978-1-4765-1630-1 (eBook PDF)
  1.  Parks, Rosa, 1913-2005—Juvenile literature. 2.  African American women—
Alabama—Montgomery—Biography—Juvenile literature. 3.  African Americans—
Alabama—Montgomery—Biography—Juvenile literature. 4.  Civil rights workers—
Alabama—Montgomery—Biography—Juvenile literature. 5.  African Americans—
Civil rights—Alabama—Montgomery—History—20th century—Juvenile literature.
6.  Segregation in transportation—Alabama—Montgomery—History—20th
century—Juvenile literature. 7.  Montgomery (Ala.)—Biography—Juvenile literature.
I. Title.
F334.M753P38384 2013
323.092—dc23
  [B]                                                                    2012033474

# Note to Parents and Teachers

The Great Women in History set supports national social studies
standards related to people and culture. This book describes
and illustrates Rosa Parks. The images support early readers in
understanding the text. The repetition of words and phrases helps
early readers learn new words. This book also introduces early
readers to subject-specific vocabulary words, which are defined
in the Glossary section. Early readers may need assistance to read
some words and to use the Table of Contents, Glossary, Read More,
Internet Sites, and Index sections of the book.

Printed in the United States of America in Stevens Point, Wisconsin.
092012        006937WZS13

# Table of Contents

1913

born

# Early Life

Civil rights pioneer Rosa Parks was born February 4, 1913. She was named Rosa Louise McCauley. Her parents were Leona and James McCauley. She had a younger brother named Sylvester.

1913

born

When she was 2, Rosa, Sylvester, and Leona went to live with Leona's parents in Pine Level, Alabama. Rosa's grandparents had been slaves. They taught her that all people should be treated equally.

Slaves were forced to work in cotton fields.

1913

born

Rosa was a good student. But she could only go to schools for black children. Segregation laws at the time kept white people and African Americans apart. Rosa did not agree with the laws.

◄ an African American school

1913
born

1932
marries
Raymond Parks

# Young Adult

At age 11, Rosa moved to Montgomery, Alabama. She went to school there. Rosa married Raymond Parks in 1932. He worked as a barber. Rosa and Raymond shared a dislike for segregation laws.

 a segregated water cooler

1913

born

1932

marries
Raymond Parks

Rosa and Raymond belonged to the National Association for the Advancement of Colored People (NAACP). This group wanted equal rights for African Americans. Rosa worked as the group's secretary in Montgomery.

an NAACP meeting

1913
born

1932
marries
Raymond Parks

1955
refuses to give
up bus seat

# Life's Work

Laws in some states said
African Americans could sit
only in the back of a bus. One day
in 1955, a bus driver asked Rosa
to give her seat to a white man.
But Rosa refused to move.

 a segregated bus

1913

born

1932

marries
Raymond Parks

1955

refuses to give
up bus seat

16

The bus driver had Rosa arrested. She was fined $10. Rosa's arrest led black people in her town to boycott riding city buses. For one year, African Americans did not ride city buses in Montgomery.

Rosa was fingerprinted by the police.

1913
born

1932
marries
Raymond Parks

1955
refuses to give
up bus seat

Rosa took her case to
the U.S. Supreme Court.
In 1956 the court decided
segregation on public buses
was against the law. Rosa won
her case.

1956

wins Supreme
Court case

1913

born

1932

marries
Raymond Parks

1955

refuses to give
up bus seat

# Remembering Rosa

Rosa spent her life working for equal rights. In 1996 she received the Presidential Medal of Freedom. Rosa died October 24, 2005, at age 92. People remember her as the "Mother of the Civil Rights Movement."

1956 — wins Supreme Court case

1996 — receives Medal of Freedom

2005 — dies

# Glossary

**arrest**—to stop and hold someone who may have broken a law

**boycott**—to refuse to buy or use a product or service to protest something believed to be wrong or unfair

**court**—a place where judges hear legal cases

**fine**—to charge someone money for breaking a law

**law**—a rule made by the government that must be obeyed

**pioneer**—a person who is the first to do something

**right**—something one can or must do by law; civil rights are freedoms that every person should have

**segregation**—separating people because of their skin color

**U.S. Supreme Court**—the most powerful court in the United States

# Read More

**Gosman, Gillian.** *Rosa Parks.* Life Stories. New York: PowerKids Press, 2011.

**Leslie, Tonya.** *Rosa Parks: A Life of Courage.* People of Character. Minneapolis: Bellwether Media, 2008.

**Linde, Barbara M.** *Rosa Parks.* Civil Rights Crusaders. New York: Gareth Stevens, 2012.

# Internet Sites

FactHound offers a safe, fun way to find Internet sites related to this book. All of the sites on FactHound have been researched by our staff.

Here's all you do:

Visit *www.facthound.com*

Type in this code: 9781620650714

Check out projects, games and lots more at
**www.capstonekids.com**

# Index

Word Count: 296
Grade: 1
Early-Intervention Level: 24

**Editorial Credits**
Erika L. Shores, editor; Alison Thiele, designer; Wanda Winch, media researcher;
Jennifer Walker, production specialist

**Photo Credits**
AP Images, cover; Birmingham, Ala. Public Library Archives, File #1556.49.59, 14;
Corbis: Bettmann, 4, 18; Library of Congress: Prints and Photographs Division, 1,
6, 8, 10, 12, 16; National Archives and Records Administration, 20; Shutterstock:
yienkeat, bus design element

3/14 ③